To: Ryan & Noel
From: Alexandria Hilton and
Rick Herrington

To Love
& Cherish

31 August 2013

Dear Ryan and Noel

Wishing you a long, joyful and fulfilling life together. Welcome to your new home! Enjoy the magic of the house and setting! Warmest regards

Elizabeth
Colwell

To Love & Cherish

Poetry, Prose and Blessings for Love and Marriage

Victoria Jean Kinloch

ROBINSON

Robinson Publishing
7, Kensington Church Court, London W8 4SP

ISBN 1-85487-878-6

Printed in China

9 8 7 6 5 4 3 2 1

FOR
Veronica and Frank,
Wendy and John
Candie and K. J.—
What Greater Thing?

Contents

Introduction   6

I   **How Do I Love Thee?**   7
In Praise of Love

II   **With These Words**   17
Vows, Blessings and Traditions

III   **Whither Thou Goest**   33
Readings for the Bride

IV   **Come Live With Me**   43
Readings for the Groom

V   **What Greater Thing?**   55
Readings for Family and Friends

Introduction

Some of our best-loved poems, prose, traditions and rituals praise married love, the culmination of romantic love. Transcending barriers of culture, race and religion, love in its essence is known to all. Falling in love inspires joy, tenderness and wonder—intangible feelings that writers through the ages have tried to capture in words, but the depth and breadth of true love is known only to the lovers. From the first flirtatious glances, to the first kiss, to the declaration of their mutual feelings, romantic love begins as a private celebration.

The marriage ceremony is one of the greatest events in love's journey. At once solemn and joyful, it comprises words, music and sacred symbols that are meaningful to the engaged couple and their loved ones. These elements can be chosen from a myriad of traditions, to make the ceremony uniquely personal. Or they may be as traditional as the moving vows from The Book of Common Prayer: "With this ring I thee wed, with my body I thee worship, and with all my wordly goods I thee endow."

The reception that follows the ceremony has its own diverse customs, from the newlyweds' first dance together to the shared cutting of the wedding cake. Toasts, tributes and blessings all mark this occasion as a time to rejoice, not only in the union of this unique couple, but in the greatest gift of all.

How Do
I Love Thee?

IN PRAISE OF LOVE

BETROTHALS

As True a Heart

Accept, my love, as true a heart
  As ever lover gave:
'Tis free, it vows, from any art,
  And proud to be your slave.

Then take it kindly, as 'twas meant,
  And let the giver live,
Who, with it, would the world have sent,
  Had it been his to give.

    ∞ MATTHEW PRIOR

A Betrothal

Put your hand on my heart,
Say that you love me as
The woods upon the hills cleave to the hills' contours.

    ∞ E.J. SCOVELL

Like a Singing Bird

My heart is like a singing bird
    Whose nest is in a watered shoot;
My heart is like an apple-tree
    Whose boughs are bent with thick-set fruit;
My heart is like a rainbow shell
    That paddles in a halcyon sea;
My heart is gladder than all these
    Because my love is come to me.

      FROM "MY HEART IS LIKE A SINGING BIRD"
        CHRISTINA ROSSETTI

One Voice

Everything that touches us, me and you,
Takes us together like a violin's bow,
Which draws one voice out of two separate strings.
Upon what instrument are we two spanned?
And what musician holds us in his hand?
O, sweetest song!

      FROM "LOVE SONG"
        RAINER MARIA RILKE

Now Touch the Air Softly

I'll love you till Heaven
Rips the stars from his coat,
And the Moon rows away in
A glass-bottomed boat;
And Orion steps down
Like a diver below,
And Earth is ablaze,
And Ocean aglow.

∞ WILLIAM JAY SMITH

The Yüeh-Fu

I want to be your soulmate
for all eternity.
When the mountains are flat
and the rivers run dry,
when the trees blossom in winter
and the snow falls in summer,
when heaven and earth are one—
Only then will we two be parted.

∞ CHINESE FOLK BALLAD

1ST CENTURY BC

LOVE'S CELEBRATION

Love Divine

Nothing is sweeter than love; nothing stronger,
nothing higher, nothing wider; nothing happier,
nothing fuller, nothing better in heaven and earth.

∾ THOMAS À KEMPIS

Only We

Lip on lip, and eye to eye,
Love to love, we live, we die;
No more thou, and no more I,
    We, and only we!

∾ RICHARD MONCKTON MILNES

Is It for Now or for Always

I take you now and for always,
For always is always now.

∾ PHILIP LARKIN

Love's Philosophy

The fountains mingle with the river
 And the rivers with the Ocean,
The winds of Heaven mix for ever
 With a sweet emotion;
Nothing in the world is single;
 All things by a law divine
In one spirit meet and mingle.
 Why not I with thine?—

    ∞ PERCY BYSSHE SHELLEY

I Love You Simply

I love you without knowing how, or when, or
 from where,
I love you simply, without problems or pride:
I love you in this way because I don't know any
 other way of loving.

   ∞ FROM "SONNET XVII"
   PABLO NERUDA

Song

*L*ove and harmony combine,
And around our souls intwine,
While thy branches mix with mine,
And our roots together join.

Joys upon our branches sit,
Chirping loud, and singing sweet;
Like gentle streams beneath our feet
Innocence and virtue meet.

Thou the golden fruit dost bear,
I am clad in flowers fair;
Thy sweet boughs perfume the air,
And the turtle buildeth there.

ᗄ WILLIAM BLAKE

So Well I Love Thee

*S*o well I love thee, as without thee I
Love nothing; if I might choose, I'd rather die
Than be one day debarr'd thy company.

ᗄ MICHAEL DRAYTON

PROCLAMATIONS

If You Will Marry Me

MIRANDA: I am your wife, if you will marry me;
    If not, I'll die your maid: to be your fellow
    You may deny me; but I'll be your servant,
    Whether you will or no.

FERDINAND: My mistress, dearest;
    And I thus humble ever.

MIRANDA: My husband, then?

FERDINAND: Ay, with a heart as willing
    As bondage e'er of freedom: here's my hand.

MIRANDA: And mine, with my heart in't.

இ FROM *The Tempest*, WILLIAM SHAKESPEARE

A Pure Heart

*B*ecause we have believed intensely and with a pure heart in the world, the world will open the arms of God to us. It is for us to throw ourselves into these arms so that the divine milieu should close around our lives like a circle.

∞ PIERRE TEILHARD DE CHARDIN

I'll Give My Love

I'll give my love an apple without a core,
I'll give my love a house without a door,
I'll give my love a palace wherein she may be,
And she may unlock it without a key.

My head is the apple without a core,
My mind is the house without a door,
My heart is the palace wherein she may be,
And she may unlock it without any key.

∞ ANONYMOUS

Infinite Love

JULIET: What satisfaction canst thou have tonight?

ROMEO: The exchange of thy love's faithful vow for mine.

JULIET: I gave thee mine before thou didst request it;
And yet I would it were to give again.

ROMEO: Wouldst thou withdraw it? for what purpose, love?

JULIET: But to be frank, and give it thee again.
And yet I wish but for the thing I have:
My bounty is as boundless as the sea,
My love as deep; the more I give to thee,
The more I have, for both are infinite.

         ✆ FROM *Romeo and Juliet*
         WILLIAM SHAKESPEARE

$\mathcal{N}$ow I know what love is.

     ✆ VIRGIL

With
These Words

VOWS, BLESSINGS AND
TRADITIONS

VOWS AND PROMISES

To Have and to Hold

I take you as my lawful wedded wife/husband; to have and to hold from this day forward; for better or worse; for richer or poorer; in sickness and in health; to love and to cherish, as long as we both shall live.

∞ TRADITIONAL CHRISTIAN VOW

Share the Joys

*Y*ou have become mine forever. Yes, we have become partners. I have become yours. Hereafter, I cannot live without you. Let us share the joys.

∞ HINDU MARRIAGE RITUAL

I Believe in Us

I believe in you as I believe in myself. Above all else, I believe in us.

Our Love is Stronger

Our love extends beyond the edges of the earth; it is greater than who we are; it is more powerful than our past; it is the solid ground upon which we stand and the air we shall breathe in our future.

You Are My Everything

You have been my yesterday, you are my today, and you will be my tomorrow.
Our past is yesterday;
Our new day is now begun;
Our present is the dawning of this new sun.

The Essence of Our Lives

Our love has brought us together before this gathering of our family, friends and community; we declare our solemn vows to honour this love for all the days to come. Our love is the essence of our lives.

Till Death Us Part

*F*or better and for worse,
Through blessing and through curse,
We shall be one, till life's last hour shall come.

 ∞ ARTHUR PENRHYN STANLEY

I Had Been Waiting for You

*W*hen I met you, I realised that I had not been truly living, but waiting. I knew then that I had been waiting for you to enter my life—to stay.

A Marriage Prayer

*S*pirit of happiness, smile upon us.
Spirit of love, bind us together.
Spirit of fertility, bless us.
Spirit of good health, favour us.
Spirit of endurance, grant us strength.
Spirit of compassion, make us kind.
Spirit of protection, guard our lives.

GESTURES OF UNION

Taking a Solemn Oath

The meaning of marriage begins in the giving of words. We cannot join ourselves to one another without giving our word. And this must be an unconditional giving, for in joining ourselves to one another we join ourselves to the unknown. We can join one another *only* by joining the unknown.

∞ WENDELL BERRY

Sharing a Loving Cup

An age-old French custom involved the bride and groom together drinking a toast from the *coupe de mariage* (a two-handled marriage cup). Often handed down through the generations, this special cup was filled after the vows were taken. Drinking from one cup symbolised the merging of their lives.

Clasping Hands

*T*he "handfasting" ritual was the traditional form of wedding ceremony for the ancient Celts. The couple would clasp hands through the hollow centre of a menhir, or standing stone, and declare themselves husband and wife before the people of their village. This form of marriage remained legally binding in Scotland until 1939.

Holding a Candle

*I*n Greek and German traditions, the love, happiness and spiritual illumination that a bride and groom bring to each other on their wedding day are symbolised by each holding a candle, brightly decorated with ribbons and flowers.

Growing Together

*A*s part of the traditional wedding ceremony in Bermuda, it is customary for the bride and groom to plant a tree together. This tree symbolises their new life together and the maturing of their love for each other.

Seven Steps

*H*indu tradition requires that the couple take seven symbolic steps before entering into matrimony. After the steps are completed, the bride and groom are publicly and privately recognised as belonging only to each other.

Love's Delicate Blossom

*D*uring the exchange of vows in Burmese wedding ceremonies, the bride and groom each hold a bouquet of flowers, symbolic of their shared commitment to nurture and protect each other. After the recitation of the vows, the bride and groom dip their hands into a bowl of water, which represents the water of life.

Crossing the Threshold

*T*he Old English tradition of the groom carrying the bride over the threshold of their new home is still widely observed today. The door symbolises a gateway to the future, and serves both as a departure from the past and an entrance to the new, shared life.

A Circle of Unity

*I*n China, traditional Buddhist weddings usually take
place in the bride's bedchamber. Adorned with bamboo
and cotton headdresses, the bride and groom sit across
from each other with the members of the wedding
party forming a circle that links them. The officiant
lights a candle and chants, invoking the gods to witness
and bless the wedding. The couple is then sprinkled
with water and instructed in the responsibilities of
marriage. A celebration follows the ceremony.

Ringing the Wedding Bells

*T*he ritual of ringing bells is both an Eastern and a
Christian tradition, symbolising mystical occurrences.
Known as the *ghanta* in Buddhism, the sacred bell is
rung to symbolise communication with spirits. In
Christian tradition, bell ringing signifies the entrance
of the Holy Spirit, and the sounding of wedding bells
declares publicly that a couple has been joined in the
sacrament of matrimony.

Love's Fragility

*B*reaking a glass underfoot is a traditional element in Jewish wedding ceremonies. The fragile glass, so easily splintered, reminds the bride and groom to love and nurture each other, protecting one another from harm.

Unveiling

*I*n many cultures, young women have worn veils before marriage, as a sign of chastity and modesty. Even where this custom is not observed, the veil is often used in the wedding ceremony. After the vows, it is symbolically lifted by the bridegroom as the bride reveals and gives herself to him.

Kissing

*A*fter the vows have been exchanged and the bride and groom declared husband and wife, they kiss before the assembled witnesses. This kiss is their first as a married couple and an open declaration and celebration of their love for each other.

SYMBOLS OF LOVE

Heart and Arrow

*T*raditionally, the heart has been regarded as the seat of the emotions, and it has long been a universal symbol of love. The arrow is the attribute of the Greek god of love, Eros (the Roman Cupid). When two hearts are depicted pierced with an arrow, it signifies both the love of two people for one another and the union it forms.

Commitment Rings

*T*he ring is given as a binding token of undying love, and worn to display the acceptance of, and commitment to, that bond. The circular shape of the ring symbolises eternity, completeness and the union of the couple. After the rings are blessed in the wedding ceremony, they are placed on the fourth finger of the left hand. Historically, it was believed that the fourth finger was connected to the heart.

Bridal Flowers

*F*lowers are an element in the wedding ceremonies of most cultures, past and present, and their symbolism adds another dimension to the celebration. Red roses signify love (for Christians, red symbolises the blood of Christ); white, innocence and purity; and yellow, friendship. When red and white roses are placed together, they demonstrate the union of opposites— in this case, the bride and groom. Chrysanthemums represent happiness, longevity, luck and wealth, and are especially symbolic in the Far East. Other popular wedding flowers include: columbines, which were an attribute of Aphrodite, the Greek goddess of love; lilies, which were sacred to the goddess Juno and, for Christians, represent the Virgin Mary—they stand for purity and motherhood in both traditions; lotus flowers, especially symbolic for Hindus (for whom they represent the goddess of beauty and good fortune, Lakshmi) and Buddhists (the sacred lotus also stands for sexual union); pansies, considered an attribute of Venus in ancient Rome, and once popularly known as "Cupid's Delight" and "Kiss-Me"; and tulips, which symbolise perfect love.

Cake

*I*t is traditional in Europe for the bride and groom to cut the wedding cake together: this represents a first step in their new life and their love and mutual responsibility for each other. This tradition has evolved further in the United States, where the first piece of cake is offered by the bride to the groom, and vice versa, to symbolise their commitment to care for each other.

Horseshoe

*T*urned upward, the horseshoe is a symbol of good luck, a belief rooted in the magical powers ascribed to the horse in many myths. It also represents fertility and vitality. Miniature horseshoes are often incorporated into the decoration of wedding cakes.

Confetti

*I*t was once a widespread custom for friends and family to shower the bride and groom with rice after the wedding ceremony, signifying fertility and abundance. Today, confetti is used, but the symbolism remains the same.

Apples

Venus used golden apples to tempt Atalanta, and Eve was seduced with an apple, which came to represent erotic love. It is also an ancient fertility symbol. Apples were used in the wedding feasts of ancient Rome and in medieval Europe, to represent the beauty of the bride—the "apple of the groom's eye."

Scallop Shells

Universal feminine symbols of birth and life, scallop shells also signify love. According to legend, the Greek goddess Aphrodite (the Roman Venus) and the Hindu goddess Lakshmi were created from sea foam and carried to shore on a scallop shell.

Welsh Love Spoon

Until the nineteenth century, it was a folk custom in Wales for a suitor to present his beloved with a carved wooden love spoon that he had crafted himself. If the spoon was accepted, they were betrothed.

Lovebirds

Releasing a pair of birds, especially turtledoves or lovebirds, during the wedding ceremony represents the love the bride and groom feel for each other and the joy they bring each other. Lovebirds, of the parakeet family, acquired their popular nickname because the bond between nesting pairs is unusually close and devoted. Until the early twentieth century, suitors in England sometimes presented a pair of lovebirds to their intended, and a similar custom still exists in parts of South America.

Key

The key signifies a transition: unlocking a door opens a new world, while locking a door behind one seals the past. For Christians, keys represent St. Peter at the gates of heaven and are also a papal emblem, and in Japan a key stands for happiness. In the context of a wedding ceremony, the key symbolises the closing of two separate lives and the opening of a new life together.

REMINDERS AND RENEWALS

To His Wife on their Fourteenth Anniversary

"*T*hee, Mary, with this ring I wed,"
So fourteen years ago I said.
Behold another ring! "For what?"
To wed thee o'er again—why not?

With the first ring I married youth,
Grace, beauty, innocence, and truth;
Taste long admired, sense long revered,
And all my Molly then appeared.

If she, by merit since disclosed,
Prove twice the woman I supposed,
I plead that double merit now,
To justify a double vow.

〜 SAMUEL BISHOP

The Newly Wedded

Now the rite is duly done,
    Now the word is spoken,
And the spell has made us one,
    Which may ne'er be broken;
Rest we, dearest, in our home,
    Roam we o'er the heather:
We shall rest, and we shall roam,
    Shall we not? together.

        WINTHROP MACKWORTH PRAED

Thou Hast Sworn by Thy God

Thou hast sworn by thy God, my Jeanie,
    By that pretty white hand o' thine,
And by a' the lowing stars in heaven,
    That thou wad aye by mine!
And I hae sworn by my God, my Jeanie,
    And by that kind heart o' thine,
By a' the stars sown thick owre heaven,
    That thou shal aye be mine!

        ALLAN CUNNINGHAM

Whither Thou Goest

READINGS FOR THE BRIDE

ENTREATIES

Ruth's Wedding Vow

Ruth said:
"Intreat me not to leave thee,
 Or to return from following after thee:
For whither thou goest, I will go,
 And where thou lodgest, I will lodge.
Thy people shall be my people,
 And thy God my God.
Where thou diest, I will die,
 And there will I be buried.
The Lord do so to me, and more also,
 If ought but death part thee and me."

   FROM THE HOLY BIBLE
    RUTH 1:16–17

My Beloved is Mine

My beloved is mine, and I am his: he feedeth among the lilies.

   FROM *The Song of Solomon*

To the Bridegroom

*I*n thine honour, my bridegroom, prosper and live;
     Let thy beauty arise and shine forth fierce;
     And the heart of thine enemies God shall pierce,
And the sins of thy youth will He forgive,
     And bless thee in increase and all thou shalt do.
     When thou settest thine hand thereto.

        JUDAH HALEVI
          TRANS. NINA DAVIS

Wilt Thou Have My Hand?

*O*h, wilt thou have my hand, Dear, to lie along
     in thine?...
Oh, must thou have my soul, Dear, commingled
     with thy soul?
Red grows the cheek, and warm the hand; the
     part is in the whole!
Nor hands nor cheeks keep separate, when soul
     is joined to soul.

        ELIZABETH BARRETT BROWNING

Necessary

I would like to be the air
that inhabits you for a moment
only. I would like to be that unnoticed
& that necessary.

> ∽ FROM "VARIATION ON THE WORD SLEEP"
> MARGARET ATWOOD

Open Thine Heart

*I*f I leave all for thee, wilt thou exchange
And be all to me?…
Alas, I have grieved so I am hard to love.
Yet love me—wilt thou? Open thine heart wide,
And fold within the wet wings of thy dove.

> ∽ FROM "IF I LEAVE ALL FOR THEE"
> ELIZABETH BARRETT BROWNING

REFLECTIONS

To My Dear and Loving Husband

*I*f ever two were one, then surely we.
If ever man were lov'd by wife, then thee;
If ever wife was happy in a man,
Compare with me ye women if you can.
I prize thy love more then whole Mines of gold,
Or all the riches that the East doth hold.
My love is such that Rivers cannot quench,
Nor ought but love from thee, give recompense.
Thy love is such I can no way repay,
The heavens reward thee manifold I pray.
Then while we live, in love lets so persever,
That when we live no more, we may live ever.

       ⌒ ANNE BRADSTREET

A Declaration

I hereby give myself. I love…absolutely with my
complete self, with all my flesh and mind and heart.

       ⌒ FROM THE BOOK AND THE BROTHERHOOD
           IRIS MURDOCH

It Was a Quiet Way

*I*t was a quiet way—
He asked if I was his—
I made no answer of the Tongue
But answer of the Eyes—
And then He bore me on
Before this mortal noise
With swiftness, as of Chariots
And distance, as of Wheels.

∽ EMILY DICKINSON

A Letter to Daphnis

*T*his to the crown and blessing of my life,
The much loved husband of a happy wife;
To him whose constant passion found the art
To win a stubborn and ungrateful heart,
And to the world by tenderest proof discovers
They err, who say that husbands can't be lovers.

∽ ANNE, COUNTESS OF WINCHILSEA

The Knowing

I am so lucky that I know him.
This is the only way to know him.
I am the only one who knows him.
When I wake again, he is still looking at me,
    as if he is eternal.

      ∞ SHARON OLDS

He is My Own Being

…*H*e's more myself than I am. Whatever our souls
are made of, his and mine are the same….If all else
perished and *he* remained, I should still continue to be,
and if all else remained, and he were annihilated, the
universe would turn to a might stranger….He's always,
always in my mind; not as a pleasure to myself, but as
my own being.

      ∞ FROM *Wuthering Heights*
      EMILY BRONTË

SURRENDER

As Happy As I Can Be

"Mr. Rochester, if ever I did a good deed in my life—
if ever I thought a good thought—if ever I prayed a
sincere and blameless prayer—if ever I wished a
righteous wish,—I am rewarded now. To be your
wife is, for me, to be as happy as I can be on earth."

꙳ FROM *Jane Eyre*, CHARLOTTE BRONTË

I Love Thee So

There is no one beside thee, and no one above thee;
Thou standest alone, as the nightingale sings!
Yet my words that would praise thee are impotent things,
For none can express thee though all should approve thee!
I love thee so, Dear, that I only can love thee.

꙳ FROM "INSUFFICIENCY"
ELIZABETH BARRETT BROWNING

The Whole of Me, Forever

Doubt me, my dim companion!
Why, God would be content
With but a fraction of the love
Poured thee without a stint.
The whole of me, forever,
What more the woman can—
Say quick, that I may dower thee
With last delight I own!

∾ FROM "SURRENDER"
EMILY DICKINSON

Sonnet XXII

When our two souls stand up erect and strong,
Face to face, silent, drawing nigh and nigher,
Until the lengthening wings break into fire
At either curvèd point,—what bitter wrong
Can the earth do to us, that we should not long
Be here contented!...

∾ FROM *Sonnets from the Portuguese*
ELIZABETH BARRETT BROWNING

Sonnet XLIII

*H*ow do I love thee? Let me count the ways.
I love thee to the depth and breadth and height
My soul can reach, when feeling out of sight
For the ends of Being and ideal Grace.
I love thee to the level of every day's
Most quiet need, by sun and candlelight.
I love thee freely, as men strive for Right;
I love thee purely, as they turn from Praise.
I love thee with the passion put to use
In my old griefs, and with my childhood's faith.
I love thee with a love I seemed to lose
With my lost saints,—I love thee with the breath,
Smiles, tears, of all my life!—and, if God choose,
I shall but love thee better after death.

FROM *Sonnets from the Portuguese*
ELIZABETH BARRETT BROWNING

Come Live With Me

READINGS FOR THE GROOM

ADORATION

She Walks in Beauty

She walks in beauty, like the night
　　Of cloudless climes and starry skies;
And all that's best of dark and bright
　　Meet in her aspect and her eyes:
Thus mellowed to that tender light
　　Which heaven to gaudy day denies.

One shade the more, one ray the less,
　　Had half impaired the nameless grace
Which waves in every raven tress,
　　Or softly lightens o'er her face;
Where thoughts serenely sweet express
　　How pure, how dear their dwelling place.

And on that cheek, and o'er that brow,
　　So soft, so calm, yet eloquent,
The smiles that win, the tints that glow,
　　But tell of days in goodness spent,
A mind at peace with all below,
　　A heart whose love is innocent!

◆ GEORGE GORDON, LORD BYRON

My Beautifullest Bride

And ye three handmayds of the Cyprian Queene,
The which doe still adorne her beauties pride,
Helpe to addorne my beautifullest bride:
And as ye her array, still throw betweene
Some graces to be seene,
And as ye use to Venus, to her sing,
The whiles the woods shal answer, and your eccho ring.

❧ FROM "EPITHALAMION" (WEDDING SONG)
EDMUND SPENSER

Before that Hour

I ne'er was struck before that hour
  With love so sudden and so sweet,
Her face it bloomed like a sweet flower
  And stole my heart away complete.

❧ FROM "FIRST LOVE"
JOHN CLARE

Heavenly Paradise

There is a garden in her face
    Where roses and white lilies blow;
A heavenly paradise is that place,
    Wherein all pleasant fruits do flow:
There cherries grow which none may buy
    Till 'Cherry-ripe' themselves do cry.

      FROM "CHERRY-RIPE"
      THOMAS CAMPION

None Like to My Lady

I have seen many that have beauty
Yet is there none like to my lady
    That ever I saw.

Therefore I dare boldly say,
I shall have the best and fairest May
    That ever I saw.

      ANONYMOUS

Shall I Compare Thee to a Summer's Day?

Shall I compare thee to a summer's day?
Thou art more lovely and more temperate:
Rough winds do shake the darling buds of May,
And summer's lease hath all too short a date:
Sometime too hot the eye of heaven shines,
And often is his gold complexion dimmed;
And every fair from fair sometime declines,
By chance, or nature's changing course untrimmed;
But thy eternal summer shall not fade,
Nor lose possession of that fair thou owest,
Nor shall death brag thou wanderest in his shade,
When in eternal lines to time thou growest;
    So long as men can breathe, or eyes can see,
    So long lives this, and this gives life to thee.

∝ "Sonnet XVIII"
    William Shakespeare

Heartfelt Delight

*T*he happiness which this reply produced was such
as he had probably never felt before; and he expressed
himself on the occasion as sensibly and warmly as a
man violently in love can be supposed to do. Had
Elizabeth been able to enounter his eye, she might
have seen how well the expression of heart-felt delight,
diffused over his face, became him; but though she
could not look, she could listen, and he told her of
feelings, which, in proving of what importance she was
to him, made his affection every moment more valuable.

⤎ FROM *Pride and Prejudice*
JANE AUSTEN

The Pledge

*W*e pledged our hearts, my love and I,
    I in my arms the maiden clasping;
I could not tell the reason why,
    But, O, I trembled like an aspen!

⤎ FROM "THE EXCHANGE"
SAMUEL TAYLOR COLERIDGE

PROPOSALS

The Passionate Shepherd to His Love

Come live with me and be my Love,
And we will all the pleasures prove
That hills and valleys, dales and fields,
Or woods or steepy mountain yields.

And we will sit upon the rocks,
And see the shepherds feed their flocks
By shallow rivers, to whose falls
Melodious birds sing madrigals.

And I will make thee beds of roses
And a thousand fragrant posies;
A cap of flowers, and a kirtle
Embroidered all with leaves of myrtle.

The shepherd swains shall dance and sing
For thy delight each May morning:
If these delights thy mind may move,
Then live with me and be my Love.

     CHRISTOPHER MARLOWE

To Celia

Drink to me only with thine eyes,
  And I will pledge with mine;
Or leave a kiss but in the cup
  And I'll not look for wine.
The thirst that from the soul doth rise
  Doth ask a drink divine;
But might I of Jove's nectar sup,
  I would not change for thine.
I sent thee late a rosy wreath,
But thou thereon didst only breathe,
  And sent'st it back to me;
Since when it grows, and smells, I swear,
  Not of itself but thee!

❧ BEN JONSON

Whole Love

*L*ove me more than dearly, love me wholly,
Love me with no weighing of circumstance,
As I am pledged in honour to love you:

With no weakness, with no speculation
On what might happen should you and I prove less
Than bringer-to-be of our own certainty.

ROBERT GRAVES

The Best Is Yet to Be

*G*row old along with me!
The best is yet to be,
The last of life, for which the first was made:
Our times are in his hand
Who saith, "A whole I planned,
Youth shows but half; trust God: see all, nor be afraid!"

FROM "RABBI BEN EZRA"
ROBERT BROWNING

PERSUASIONS

Serenity

Before I found my true love,
my heart was lost.
But now that I know her,
now that I hold her,
my heart is serene.

∞ ANCIENT CHINESE FOLK SONG

Eskimo Marriage Song

You are my wife.
My feet shall run because of you.
My feet, dance because of you.
My heart shall beat because of you.
My eyes, see because of you.
My mind, think because of you.
And I shall love because of you.

∞ TRADITIONAL

The Most Sacred Pledge

No woman can truthfully say to her lover
That any man ever loved her as I love you.
No lover bound by the most sacred pledge
Was ever found more true to his love.

        CATULLUS

A Dreame of Thee

I wonder by my troth, what thou, and I
Did, till we lov'd? were we not wean'd till then?
But suck'd on countrey pleasures, childishly?
Or snorted we in the seven sleepers' den?
'Twas so; But this, all pleasures fancies bee.
If ever any beauty I did see,
Which I desir'd, and got, 'twas but a
    dreame of thee.

      FROM "THE GOOD-MORROW"
      JOHN DONNE

Our Love Hath No Decay

All other things to their destruction draw,
    Only our love hath no decay;
This no tomorrow hath, nor yesterday,
Running it never runs from us away,
But truly keeps its first, last, everlasting day.

         ∾ FROM "THE ANNIVERSARY"
         JOHN DONNE

I Love Thee Better Now

Oh, no—not ev'n when first we lov'd
    Wert thou as dear as now thou art;
Thy beauty then my senses mov'd,
    But now thy virtues bind my heart.
What was but Passion's sign before
    Has since been turn'd to Reason's vow;
And, though I then might love thee *more*,
    Trust me, I love thee *better* now.

         ∾ FROM "OH, NO—NOT EV'N WHEN FIRST WE LOV'D"
         THOMAS MOORE

What Greater Thing?

READINGS FOR FAMILY AND FRIENDS

THANKSGIVING

Be Each Other's Comfort

God with honour hang your head,
Groom, and grace you, bride, your bed
With lissome scions, sweet scions,
Out of hallowed bodies bred.

Each be other's comfort kind:
Déep, déeper than divined,
Divine charity, dear charity,
Fast you ever, fast bind.

ॐ FROM "AT THE WEDDING MARCH"
GERARD MANLEY HOPKINS

Good Tidings

It is time to speak words of good tidings
    for the beloved bride and groom.
It is time for us to dance and celebrate and rejoice.

ॐ ARISTOPHANES

Cana's Wine

Now, if your loves will lend an ear to mine,
I toast you both, good son and dear new daughter.
May you not lack for water,
And may that water smack of Cana's wine.

> ⚮ FROM "A WEDDING TOAST"
> RICHARD WILBUR

What Greater Thing...

What greater thing is there for two human souls
than to feel that they are joined...to strengthen
each other...to be at one with each other in silent
unspeakable memories?

> ⚮ GEORGE ELIOT

Blessing

May peace around this family dwell;
Make this house happy.

> ⚮ NAVAJO

Two Bodies

Now you will feel no rain,
for each of you will be a shelter to the other.

Now you will feel no cold,
for each of you will be warmth to the other.

Now there is no loneliness for you;
now there is no more loneliness.

Now you are two bodies,
but there is only one life before you.

Go now to your dwelling place,
to enter into your days together.

And may your days be good
and long on the earth.

Apache Song

Unbroken Bond of Love

Happy are those held by an unbroken bond
of love that will not be separated before death.

Horace

DESTINY

Message in a Bride's Bouquet

God's blessing is in the beauty of a flower—
And sanctifies it for a marriage dower.
The flowers in your bouquet are not by chance
But chosen for their rich significance....

So as you take your place, a bride,
Your chosen life-mate close beside,
May Heaven and Earth and Man combine
To keep these blessings ever thine,
And give you strength to do your part
With ready hand and loyal heart.

— RACHEL PAGE ELLIOT

Lips May Mingle Souls

Now, bride and bridegroom, help to sing
The prize which Wedding here doth bring;...
And, free from all the world and noise,
May you enjoy your mutual joys;
    Now you no fear controls
    But lips may mingle souls;
    And soft embraces bind
    To each the other's mind;
    Which may no power untie,
    Till one or both must die.

         ☙ FROM "NOW, BRIDE AND BRIDEGROOM," BEN JONSON

Ephesians: 4:25–32

Husbands, love your wives as you love your own
bodies. In loving his wife a man loves himself. For
no one ever hated his own body: on the contrary, he
provides and cares for it; and thus it is that a man shall
leave his father and mother and shall be joined to his
wife and the two shall become one flesh.

    It is a great truth that is hidden here.

         ☙ FROM THE HOLY BIBLE

Love the Love

From this time, until
The time you must rejoin the
Earth from which you came,
Love the love in you that underlies
Your actions.
And with each other,
Share your wonder at the beauty
That you find
As Man and Wife.

FROM "NOT FROM PRIDE, BUT FROM HUMILITY"
JAMES LAWSON

Essence

The essence of a good marriage is respect for each
other's personality combined with that deep intimacy,
physical, mental, and spiritual, which makes a serious
love between man and woman the most fructifying of
all human experiences.

FROM "MARRIAGE AND MORALS"
BERTRAND RUSSELL

Be Thou Magnified

*B*e thou magnified, O bridegroom, like Abraham, and blessed like Isaac, and increase like Jacob, walking in peace and living in righteousness....

And thou, O bride, be magnified like Sarah, and rejoice like Rebecca, and increase like Rachel, being glad in thy husband and keeping the bounds of the law.

ᦉ FROM THE GREEK ORTHODOX MARRIAGE SERVICE

Hawaiian Wedding Song

*H*ere all seeking is over,
the lost has been found,
a mate has been found
to share the chills of winter—
now Love asks
that you be united.

Now All is One

*T*hy spouse the self-same is with thee,
In body, mind, in goods and name:
    No thine, no mine, may other call,
    Now all is one, and one is all.

          ~ FROM "NO LOVE, TO LOVE OF MAN AND WIFE"
          RICHARD EEDES

Buddhist Marriage Homily

*N*othing happens without a cause. The union of this
man and woman has not come about accidentally but is
the foreordained result of many past lives. This tie can
therefore not be broken or dissolved.

In the future, happy occasions will come as surely as
the morning. Difficult times will come as surely as
night. When things go joyously, meditate according to
the Buddhist tradition. When things go badly, meditate.
Meditation in the manner of the Compassionate
Buddha will guide your life.

To say the words "love and compassion" is easy. But
to accept that love and compassion are built upon
patience and perseverance is not easy.

*B*e united in love.

Ɑ Roman Proverb